Hola,
VENEZUELA

by Corey Anderson

CHERRY LAKE PUBLISHING • ANN ARBOR, MICHIGAN

Published in the United States of America by Cherry Lake Publishing
Ann Arbor, Michigan
www.cherrylakepublishing.com

Reading Adviser: Marla Conn MS, Ed., Literacy specialist, Read-Ability, Inc.

Book Design: Book Buddy Media

Photo Credits: ©omersukrugoksu/Getty Images, cover (top); ©Elizabeth Fernandez/Getty Images, cover (bottom); ©medinaalfaro/Pixabay, 1; ©Stockbyte/Getty Images, 3; ©apomares/Getty Images, 4; ©Brad Wilson, DVM/Getty Images, 5 (top); ©iStockphoto/Getty Images, 5 (bottom); ©GeoNova Maps/Getty Images, 6; ©EyeEm/Getty Images, 7; ©EyeEm/Getty Images, 8; ©María Z Rodríguez/Getty Images, 9; ©Photononstop RF/Getty Images, 10; ©Cavan Images RF/Getty Images, 11; ©500px Prime/Getty Images, 12; ©Cate Gillon/Getty Images, 13; ©National Art Gallery/Wikimedia, 14; ©Mario Tama/Getty Images, 16 (top); ©visual7/Getty Images, 16 (bottom); ©500px/Getty Images, 17; ©Edilzon Gamez/Getty Images, 18; ©Enrique Rivas/Getty Images, 19; ©Edilzon Gamez/Getty Images, 20; ©Michael Freeman/Getty Images, 21; ©Juan Silva/Getty Images, 22; ©skynesher/Getty Images, 23; ©Cristóbal Alvarado Minic/Getty Images, 24; ©The Photographer/Wikimedia, 25; ©FSTOPLIGHT/Getty Images, 26; ©Wojtek Zagorski/Getty Images, 27; ©Eric Espada/Getty Images, 28; ©Doug Benc/Getty Images, 29; ©Juan Silva/Getty Images, 30; ©Humberto Ramirez/Getty Images, 31; ©Kimberly White/Getty Images, 32; ©Erik Gonzalez Garcia/Getty Images, 33; ©EyeEm/Getty Images, 34; ©iStockphoto/Getty Images, 35; ©jmsilva/Getty Images, 36; ©iStockphoto/Getty Images, 37; ©iStockphoto/Getty Images, 38; ©apomares/Getty Images, 39; ©iStockphoto/Getty Images, 39; ©iStockphoto/Getty Images, 40; ©James Baigrie/Getty Images, 41; ©iStockphoto/Getty Images, 42; ©ALEAIMAGE/Getty Images, 43; ©Elizabeth Fernandez/Getty Images, 44; ©iStockphoto/Getty Images, 44; ©filo/Getty Images, background

Library of Congress Cataloging-in-Publication Data has been filed and is available at catalog.loc.gov

Cherry Lake Publishing would like to acknowledge the work of The Partnership for 21st Century Learning. Please visit www.p21.org for more information.

Printed in the United States of America
Corporate Graphics

TABLE OF CONTENTS

CHAPTER 1

WELCOME TO VENEZUELA!

Can you imagine a country where snowy mountains, bustling cities, stunning Caribbean beaches, and Amazonian jungles can all be found within its borders? Where animals ranging from howler monkeys to giant otters roam free? Where the world's tallest waterfall wows anyone who is lucky enough to catch a glimpse of it? This is Venezuela, a country famous for its diversity of natural attractions and stunning wildlife. It is also a place that blends the culture and heritage of its people's Caribbean, Amazonian, and Andean roots, making Venezuela a vibrant and colorful South American nation.

Venezuela's capital is Caracas. It is the most populous city in the country.

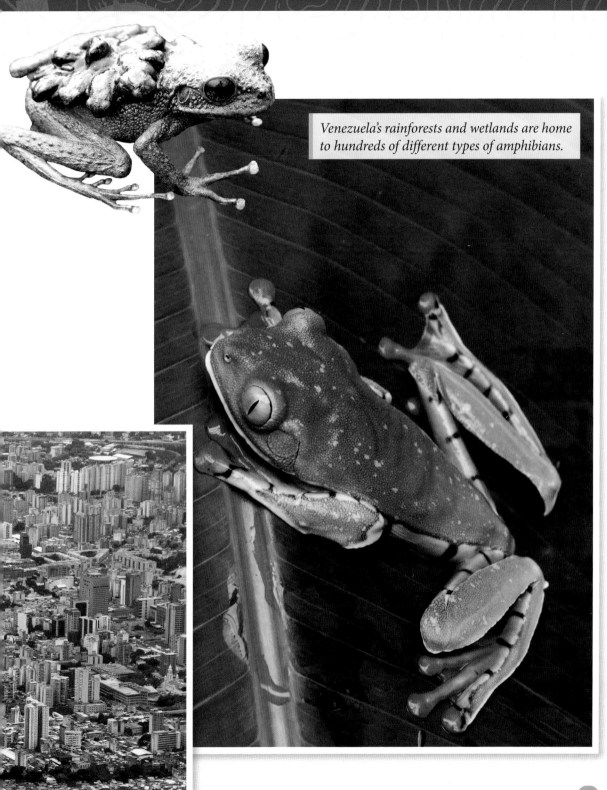

Venezuela's rainforests and wetlands are home to hundreds of different types of amphibians.

ACTIVITY

Venezuela is made up of 23 states, a capital district, and **federal** dependencies. Using a separate sheet of paper, trace the map. Use an atlas or find a map online and label each of the 23 states. Do you notice that some states are small while others are large? Why do you think this might be?

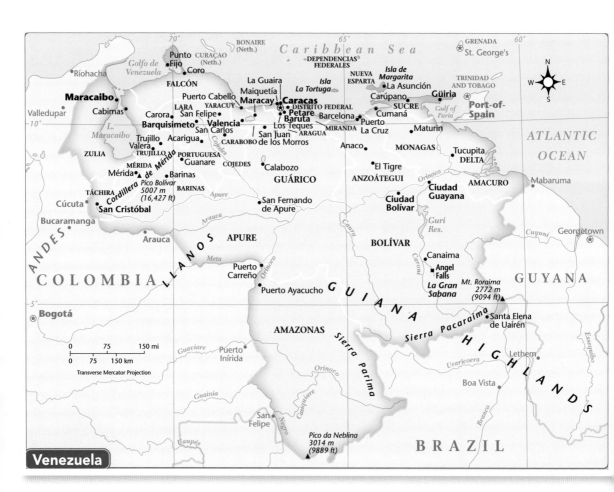

Venezuela is the sixth-largest country by area in South America. It is approximately two times the size of the state of California. The largest cities in Venezuela by population are the capital city, Caracas, and Maracaibo. About 5 million Venezuelans live in Caracas, which has a reputation for being a dangerous city where crime is common, especially in its poor neighborhoods.

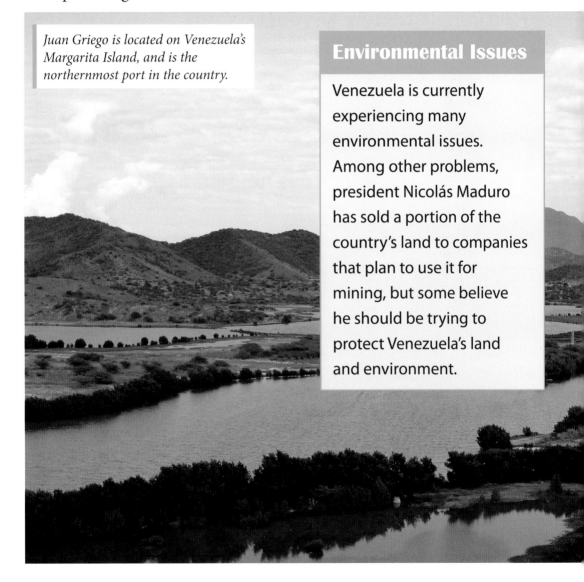

Juan Griego is located on Venezuela's Margarita Island, and is the northernmost port in the country.

Environmental Issues

Venezuela is currently experiencing many environmental issues. Among other problems, president Nicolás Maduro has sold a portion of the country's land to companies that plan to use it for mining, but some believe he should be trying to protect Venezuela's land and environment.

There are four different regions of Venezuela—the Guiana Highlands, the Orinoco lowlands, the northern mountains, and the Lake Maracaibo lowlands. Each of these regions has unique geographical features. Venezuela has the longest coastline in the Caribbean, meaning it's famous for not only its beautiful beaches, but also its islands. In fact, 72 different islands belong to Venezuela. Some are large and are home to many people, while others are just rock formations. Venezuela also features many impressive lakes. Lake Maracaibo is about 6,300 square miles (16,300 square kilometers) in size, making it the largest **inland** body of water in South America.

Venezuela is home to many impressive bodies of water, including the river Rio Orinoco, which is about 1,700 miles (2,740 km) long.

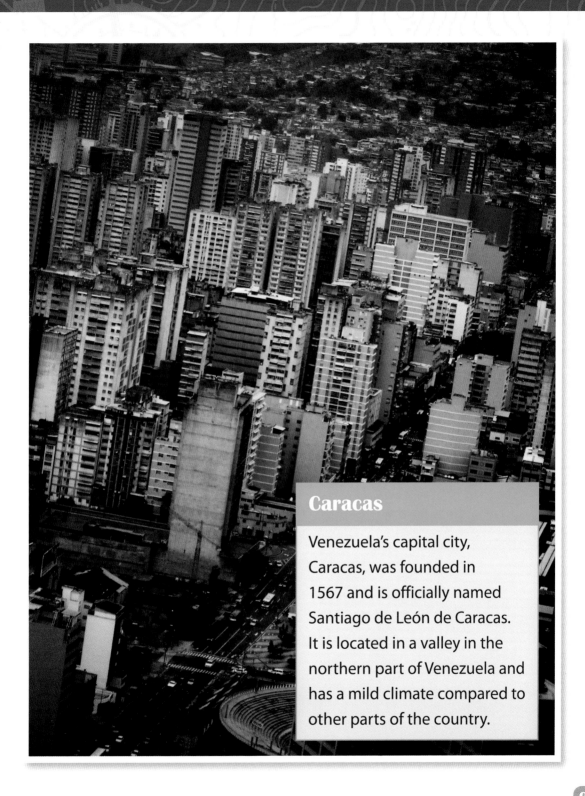

Caracas

Venezuela's capital city, Caracas, was founded in 1567 and is officially named Santiago de León de Caracas. It is located in a valley in the northern part of Venezuela and has a mild climate compared to other parts of the country.

Given its location close to the equator, Venezuela has a tropical climate. That means that temperatures across the country don't change drastically with the seasons. But, in the area closer to the Andes Mountains, it does get cooler than other regions. Up high in the mountains themselves, there are permanent patches of snow, and average temperatures only reach the mid-40s degrees Fahrenheit (7–8 degrees Celsius).

The warmest areas of Venezuela are near its coast and its lowlands. These regions are at lower altitudes, which makes them warmer than the more mountainous areas.

Margarita Island is also known as the "Isle of Pearls." Christopher Columbus arrived at this island in 1498.

Visitors sometimes travel to Venezuela's natural sulfur springs.

Venezuela has two distinct seasons. The wet season is May through November, which people in Venezuela consider to be their winter. During the wet season, sometimes it rains so hard that flooding happens, which is very destructive and dangerous. The dry summer season in Venezuela is December through April.

Venezuela is famous for its biodiversity. Biodiversity means there are a wide range of animals and plants that make the land and waters of Venezuela their home. It is estimated that there are more than 1,400 bird species, 300 types of mammals, and nearly 1,000 species of fish that can be found in Venezuela. Unusual animals that live in Venezuela include pumas and river dolphins.

Majestic Angel Falls

At 3,212 feet (979 meters) tall, Angel Falls is the world's tallest uninterrupted waterfall. It's twice as tall as the Empire State Building! To see Angel Falls in person, visitors take planes and sometimes motorized canoes to reach the waterfall's base.

CHAPTER 2

BUSINESS AND GOVERNMENT IN VENEZUELA

Historically one of the richest countries in South America, more recently Venezuela has been experiencing an economic crisis. With abundant natural oil resources, it had a booming economy in the 1970s. Political unrest, poorly managed resources, and the fall of oil prices contributed to Venezuela's economic problems.

Citizens of Venezuela often form protests to speak out against things they do not agree with.

Today, Venezuela is plagued by many issues, including soaring inflation rates. Inflation happens when the value of money decreases, so goods and services cost more. The economic crisis has also led to shortages of things like food and necessities, such as toilet paper and soap.

Venezuela's Independence

Europeans colonized Venezuela in 1522. Spanish explorers' first permanent settlement in South America was in Venezuela. Venezuela tried to gain its independence several times over the next 300 years. Then, in 1830, Venezuela finally gained permanent independence as a nation.

Oil makes up more than 90 percent of Venezuela's **exported** products. The country's financial success is very dependent on oil. This makes the economy vulnerable when the prices of oil go down. In 2017, Venezuela shipped nearly $30 billion worth of goods around the world. But that number was down more than 66 percent from what it exported just a few years earlier.

TOP EXPORTS OF VENEZUELA:

Mineral fuels, including oil: $26.6 billion

Organic chemicals: $532.6 million

Iron and steel: $350.8 million

Ores, slag, and ash: $333.4 million

Aluminum: $327.5 million

Fertilizers: $173.9 million

Fish: $151.6 million

Inorganic chemicals: $135.8 million

Copper: $60.3 million

Plastics and plastic articles: $60.1 million

0	20%	40%	60%	80%	100%

Venezuela **imports** a lot of goods from other countries. It receives the most imports from the United States annually. Venezuela is dependent on the imports of food and consumer goods products, including cereals (grains), which are the third most imported type of product into the country.

Simple groceries like pasta often are very expensive in Venezuela due to inflation.

The Flag's Symbolism

The flag of Venezuela was made official in 1836. The colors all have special meanings. Red symbolizes courage, blue symbolizes independence from Spain, and yellow symbolizes wealth. The different **provinces** of Venezuela are represented by the flag's eight stars.

ACTIVITY

Bar graphs are a good way to compare different values. Make a bar graph to show how many people have jobs related to services, industry, or agriculture in Venezuela. Ask an adult for help if you need it.

Services are jobs in which people serve others. Service jobs include teachers, police officers, and chefs. Industry means jobs extracting raw materials from land, including mining. Agriculture includes jobs in farming.

In your bar graph, use the percentages mentioned below. Which bars are closest in size? Which is the smallest? Theorize about why some job types have more workers than others.

Services: 67 percent work in services

Industry: 23 percent work in industry

Agriculture: 10 percent work in agriculture

There are many beautiful towns in Venezuela situated on the Caribbean Sea.

Today, many people view the government of Venezuela as being in crisis. Fair **democratic** practices are being abandoned as the government gains more power. People who oppose the leadership often face harsh punishments.

Venezuela's Presidency

In 2018, Nicolás Maduro was re-elected as president of Venezuela. But electoral **fraud** and poor voter turnout may have impacted the results. Voter turnout was only around 46 percent due to people who oppose Maduro boycotting the election. In January 2019, opposition leader Juan Guaidó publically swore an oath to serve as Venezuela's **interim** president. Though Maduro still officially held the title, Guaidó was recognized as Venezuela's rightful leader by the United States, Canada, and many other countries around the world.

There are 41 ports located in Venezuela.

In the early 1900s, Venezuela was led by a **dictator** named Juan Vicente Gómez. During this time, the country became the largest oil exporter in the world. After decades of military rule, a **coup** established a democratic government. But the democratic way of life didn't last long, as the country's first president was overthrown in 1948 by the military just 8 months after taking office.

The country did enjoy another period of democracy starting in the late 1950s. It also enjoyed economic success in the 1970s. But in the late 1990s, a military colonel named Hugo Chávez was elected, and led as an **authoritarian**. That means he concentrated power in the government, and jailed or punished people who opposed him. After Hugo Chávez died, the political troubles in the country continued. Today, many Venezuelans are fleeing the country to live elsewhere.

Hugo Chávez was president of Venezuela from 1998 until 2013.

Many Venezuelans are unhappy with the country's current political climate.

CHAPTER 3

MEET THE PEOPLE

The people of Venezuela come from many different places. Most of the people in the country are a mixture of **indigenous**, or native, people and Spanish. They are called *mestizos*. Spanish influence is seen throughout the culture of Venezuela in things like its food and the popularity of bullfighting. The diverse nature of the country comes to life in everything from sports to music.

Due to issues like food shortages, some families in Venezuela are moving to neighboring countries, like Colombia.

People from countries all over the world moved to Venezuela in the 20th century during the country's oil boom. Many people from China, the Middle East, and Europe traveled to Venezuela looking to get rich. Africans also came to Venezuela. Today, most Venezuelans live in cities instead of **rural** areas, and the majority of the country's population is based in the north.

Venezuelans are known for being friendly and welcoming. They often greet each other with an *abrazo*, which is a mixture of a hug and a handshake.

It is common to see people greeting each other with an abrazo.

About 3 percent of Venezuela's population are indigenous people who descended from the land's native peoples. Indigenous people face many challenges, including having their land used by others for illegal mining. Illegal mining creates environmental issues, such as polluted waters. Indigenous people also deal with many health issues, including a higher rate of infant deaths and a higher rate of HIV/AIDS infections than the larger population of Venezuela.

There are more than 1,400 different types of bird species in Venezuela, including the vibrant scarlet ibis.

VENEZUELAN ANCESTRY

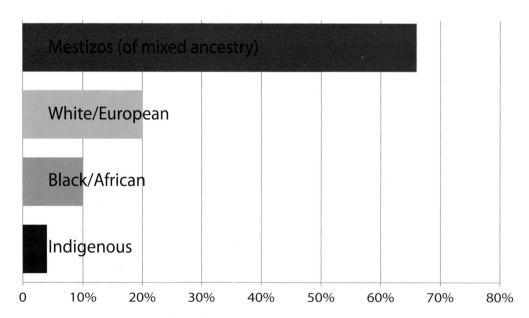

Mestizos (of mixed ancestry)

White/European

Black/African

Indigenous

0   10%   20%   30%   40%   50%   60%   70%   80%

There are 47 total public and private universities located in Venezuela.

In Venezuela, 9 years of school are **mandatory** for all children. In ninth grade, students choose to continue their studies with a focus on either humanities or sciences. This is part of Venezuela's policy to support diversified education, meaning education about different, unique topics. After middle school, students may choose to continue for 2 years of secondary school. Completing studies in technical schools, which train students in specific jobs, is becoming more popular as the industrial economy grows.

When you explore Venezuela, you may hear many different languages spoken. In fact, about 40 different languages are spoken there. Although the official language of the country is Spanish, it's not uncommon to hear Italian, Arabic, Chinese, Portuguese, or English. Some English words have been woven into the Spanish that Venezuelans speak every day. Some languages of indigenous people are becoming less common, but are still spoken in some areas.

About 11 percent of Venezuela's population live in rural areas.

ACTIVITY

The Guajiro language is a type of Arawakan language, which is spoken mostly in northern Colombia and Venezuela. It is spoken by more than 200,000 people in those two countries, and the use of this language is increasing today. Learn to count in Guajiro!

one wane (wah-neh)

two piama (pee-ah-mah)

three apünüin (ah-pu-nu-een)

four pienchi (pee-en-chee)

five járali (jah-rah-lee)

six aippirua (ah-ee-pee-oo-ruh)

seven akarachi (ah-kah-rah-chi)

eight mekiisat (meh-kee-ee-saht)

nine mekietsat (meh-kee-eht-saht)

ten poloo (poh-loh)

Found in Venezuela and elsewhere, the green iguana can reach up to 6.5 feet (2 m) long and often weighs more than 10 pounds (4.5 kg).

Popular sports in Venezuela include bullfighting, soccer, and baseball. Many of Venezuela's best baseball players eventually go on to play in Major League Baseball (MLB) in the United States. A traditional pastime that many Venezuelans love is *bolas criollas*. Similar to bocce ball, *bolas criollas* is a sport in which teams of players toss a set of balls as close as they can to a smaller target ball.

Venezuela's soccer team is nicknamed "Vino Tinto" (red wine) because of the traditional burgundy color of their jerseys.

Felix Hernandez has pitched for his home country during the World Baseball Classic.

Baseball

Miguel Cabrera and Félix Hernández are two famous Major League Baseball (MLB) players originally from Venezuela. Nicknamed "Miggy," Miguel Cabrera is a first baseman who has been an MLB All-Star 11 times! Félix Hernández is an MLB pitcher originally from Valencia, Venezuela. He threw the first "perfect game" in Seattle Mariners history, which means he pitched a whole game without an opponent reaching a base.

CHAPTER 4

CELEBRATIONS

Festival and holidays in Venezuela are heavily influenced by a blend of Spanish, indigenous, and Caribbean culture and traditions. They commemorate a wide variety of occasions. Venezuelans love to celebrate all year long, and colorful floats, music, and street parties are common among the festivities.

The Venezuelan version of April Fools' Day is celebrated on December 28th.

The Cave of the Holy Virgin is located in Morrocoy National Park.

HOLIDAYS AND CELEBRATIONS

Festival de Virgen de Coromoto (January) – Celebrates the patroness of Venezuela, who called on the world to be baptized.

Carúpano Carnival (40 days before Easter) – A giant street party featuring colorful floats and people wearing flamboyant costumes.

Fiesta de San Juan (June) – Celebrates St. John the Baptist's birth with 3 days of African drum-playing and dancing.

Día de Los Inocentes (December) – A day filled with fun, games, and practical jokes.

ACTIVITY

Make a drum like the kinds that revelers play at Fiesta de San Juan.

MATERIALS:

- An empty tin can
- Scissors
- A deflated balloon
- Beads
- Two dowel rods
- Decorative ribbon tape
- A rubber band

STEPS:

1. Cut the bottom stem portion of the balloon.

2. Stretch the balloon over the open side of the empty tin can. Put a rubber band over the edge of the balloon to keep it in place.

3. Use the decorative tape to decorate the empty tin can. Make it very colorful!

4. Add a bead to the end of each dowel rod. Those are your drum sticks.

5. Make some music!

The Dancing Devils of Corpus Christi is a set of religious festivals celebrated in Venezuela.

Carnival is celebrated all over Venezuela, with some of the most popular celebrations held in the town of El Callao.

There are several different religions practiced in Venezuela. More than 84 percent of Venezuelan citizens are Catholic. Protestant Christianity is also common, with about 4 percent identifying as Protestant. Santería is practiced by about 1 percent of Venezuelans. Santería is a mix of Native American and African religions and Christianity. About 3 percent of the country follow other religions, including Judaism, Buddhism, and Islam. More than 11 percent of Venezuelans identify as agnostic or atheist—that is, they don't practice any religion.

Iglesia de Santa Eduvigis is a beautiful church in Caracas.

Given its religious population, there are many different cathedrals and churches to be found across Venezuela.

Christmas in Venezuela is very popular. Although sometimes families display a Christmas tree in their homes, they are often artificial. Real Christmas trees are uncommon in Venezuela.

Many people across the country head to Midnight Mass at their church in the evenings leading up to Christmas. In the capital of Caracas, it is common for people to roller-skate to the morning church services from December 16 to December 24. Big presents are exchanged at midnight on Christmas Eve.

Venezuelans were introduced to Catholicism by Spaniards when they colonized the area in the 1500s.

Traditional Christmas food in Venezuela includes pan de jamón *(ham bread),* baked pig, *and* hallacas.

There are many popular foods eaten during Christmastime in Venezuela. One common Christmas food is *hallaca*, which combines a wide range of ingredients, including capers, pork, beef, raisins, and olives, that are wrapped up in plantain leaves or maize, and then steamed.

CHAPTER 5

WHAT'S FOR DINNER?

Venezuelan **cuisine** is known for blending the spices and flavors of many different cultures, including Spanish, French, West African, and Italian. Although the popularity of certain dishes varies in different regions, common ingredients in Venezuelan foods include plantains, yams, corn, and rice.

An arepa *is a cornmeal cake filled with ingredients like meat, olives, and vegetables that is then cooked on a grill.*

Consisting of pulled meat and beans, pabellón criollo is considered the national dish of Venezuela.

The popular pan de jamón is a savory pastry filled with olives and ham.

Along Venezuela's long coastline, seafood is popular. Shellfish and fish are highlighted in dishes like fish stews and soups. In the Andean region, *arepas*—small, flat bread rolls—are frequently enjoyed. There, they are often made with wheat instead of the usual cornmeal. Trout dishes are also popular in that region, made with fish from the region's streams and lakes. In the Amazon area of Venezuela, unusual ingredients may even include turtles or ants.

RECIPE

Quesillo is the Venezuelan version of a flan. It's a custard with a rich caramel topping. This recipe works with either an 8-cup (2-liter) mold or individual molds. Have an adult supervise the making of the *quesillo*, especially while dealing with hot ingredients.

INGREDIENTS:

- 3/4 cup (150 grams) sugar
- 6 large eggs
- 1 can sweetened condensed milk
- 1 cup (240 milliliters) whole milk
- 1 teaspoon (5 ml) vanilla extract
- Pinch of salt

INSTRUCTIONS

1. Melt the sugar with 2 tablespoons (30 ml) of water in a heavy saucepan over medium heat. Stir until the sugar has melted and starts to turn light brown.

2. Pour the caramelized sugar into your mold—but be careful, it's hot! Mix it around to make sure the sides and bottoms of the mold are covered.

3. Preheat oven to 325°F (163°C). Boil a small pot of water. In a bowl, whisk the eggs, condensed milk, whole milk, vanilla, and salt together.

4. Pour the egg mixture into the mold. Put the mold inside a pan with tall sides. Put the pan on the oven rack, and fill the pan with boiling water, but don't cover the mold.

5. Bake about 20 to 30 minutes, until the flan doesn't jiggle much in the middle.

6. Enjoy!

Quesillo is a popular sweet treat enjoyed in Venezuela.

Street Foods

Arepas are probably the most common street food in Venezuela, but *cachapas* are also very popular. *Cachapas* are a pancake-like cake made with corn batter. Handmade cheese is used as a stuffing, and *cachapas* are served with corn or butter on top.

Foods like arepas are found in restaurants and on street corners, sold by vendors all over Venezuela.

There are many dishes that are well loved by Venezuelans. *Arepas* are maybe the most iconic of Venezuelan foods. These bread rolls are typically made with cornmeal, then cut in half and stuffed with ingredients ranging from beef to eggs. For breakfast, Venezuelans might enjoy *pisca andina*. *Pisca andina* is a chicken broth–based soup that is filled with things like potatoes or eggs. Venezuelans often enjoy *tajadas* as a side dish with many different types of meals. *Tajadas* are fried plantain slices that get their sweet taste from the caramelization that happens while cooking them. Another famous Venezuelan snack are *empanadas*. *Empanadas* are pockets made of corn flour, filled with ingredients like ham or chicken, and then baked or fried. The national dish of Venezuela is *pabellón criollo*. This extremely popular food is made with pulled beef, rice, and black beans. To top off the meal, it's often served alongside fried plantains. Delicious!

Arepas are often used in the place of bread in Venezuela.

The popular seafood dish ceviche is enjoyed in Venezuela. It includes ingredients like chopped raw fish, lemon, onion, and sweet pepper.

There's a food shortage happening in Venezuela right now, but the restaurant scene in Caracas is still lively. The restaurants in Caracas serve everything from traditional Venezuelan foods to **fusion** cuisines to Pan-Asian fare. It's a good city to explore for adventurous eaters. Even though Venezuela is going through a tough time currently, it's a country rich with friendly people, interesting culture, beautiful landscapes, and amazing animals.

Venezuela Desserts

Beloved desserts in Venezuela include *bienmesabe*, a decadent treat that includes layers of sponge cake and coconut cream. Venezuela's version of *dulce de leche* is called *arequipe*. It is a rich caramel sauce that tops cakes or is used as a dip for fruit.

To help with expensive grocery costs, some Venezuelans are now buying vegetables straight from farmers.

GLOSSARY

authoritarian *(uh-thor-ih-TAIR-ee-un)* a type of government that doesn't allow personal freedoms

cuisine *(kwi-ZEEN)* a style or way of cooking or presenting food

democractic *(dem-uh-KRA-tik)* describing a political system in which the people elect leaders to represent them in government

dictator *(DIK-tay-tur)* a person who has complete control of a government

exported *(EK-spor-ted)* sold and shipped to another country

federal *(FED-ur-uhl)* having to do with a system in which states have their own governments but are also united under one central power

imports *(IM-ports)* brings in from another country

indigenous *(en-DIJ-en-uhs)* people native to a specific area

interim *(IN-tur-im)* accepted temporarily, to be replaced with a permanent solution at a later date

mandatory *(MAN-duh-tor-ee)* required

provinces *(PROV-inss-ez)* large parts of a country

rural *(RUR-uhl)* having to do with the country or farming

FOR MORE INFORMATION

BOOKS

Borngraber, Elizabeth. *The People and Culture of Venezuela.* Celebrating Hispanic Diversity. New York: PowerKids Press, 2018.

Orr, Tamra. *Venezuelan Heritage.* Celebrating Diversity in My Classroom. Ann Arbor: Cherry Lake Publishing, 2019.

Willis, Terri. *Venezuela.* Enchantment of the World. New York: Children's Press, 2013.

WEB SITES

Britannica—Venezuela
https://www.britannica.com/place/Venezuela
Learn more about Venezuela and its people, economy, government, and more in this informative article by Britannica.

Ducksters™ Education Site—Geography for Kids: Venezuela
https://www.ducksters.com/geography/country.php?country=Venezuela
Explore quick stats about Venezuela's people, economy, and geography.

INDEX

ABOUT THE AUTHOR

Corey Anderson is a writer and editor based in the Los Angeles area. When not typing away at a computer, Corey enjoys exploring Southern California with her two sons and husband, and participating in running races and other athletic pursuits.